EVERYTHING WE NEED

POEMS FROM EL CAMINO

Everything We Need

Poems from El Camino

Laura Foley

Headmistress Press

ISBN 978-1-7358236-9-0

Cover art: Clara Giménez © 2018, Entering Campos de Castilla.
Cover & book design by Mary Meriam.

PUBLISHER
Headmistress Press
60 Shipview Lane
Sequim, WA 98382
Telephone: 917-428-8312
Email: headmistresspress@gmail.com
Website: headmistresspress.blogspot.com

FOR CLARA

CONTENTS

FOREWORD

When they decided to walk the Camino de Santiago together, it was inevitable that Laura's poems and Clara's photos would follow. The Camino is a network of five-hundred miles of pathways winding westward through the remote villages and towns of northern Spain to the shrine of Saint James. It's been walked by pilgrims over centuries—some seeking forgiveness of sins, others for the challenge or to connect with nature.
For Laura, the trek was a poetic mission. What I find in these poems is the inspired soul of a poet who walked those many miles, as she explains: "We feel no mystic pull toward Santiago, / but we believe in the awe of those who do." These poems display all of the fragrant roses, camaraderie, and the "light moving on a shadowed field like the finger of fate," along with the weariness and aching knees. And by the end of the journey, she reports: "[H]ow strong we came to feel; how quiet inside." It is the lived experiences of Laura Foley that attracted us at Headmistress Press to *Everything We Need,* now the fourth book of hers that we have published. The experiences go hand in hand with the ability to take us along on her journeys with her deft descriptions, expansive vistas, and gentle tugs towards a more meaningful life.

We welcome you to walk this journey with Laura and Clara. You too will be strengthened by their adventure.

Risa Denenberg
Headmistress Press
February, 2022

PACKING LIGHT

Slung across my shoulders,
I will walk with it across Vermont,
then the Pyrenees, along a rutted, ancient
Roman road. Not too heavy,
I will carry its silent weight
through noisy Pamplona, Burgos, Léon,
across the flat *Meseta,* whose dry heat
cooks my feet in sturdy shoes,
through soothing wooded mountains,
valleys of Galicia. My not-young knees
will carry us through Spanish wilderness
and time—Isabella's shadow,
Charlemagne's too, Teresa of Avila's,
St. James', of course, to Compostela,
Meadow of the Stars.
Step by step, from east to west,
beneath the glittering milky way,
through history, and back to possible futures,
my purple backpack and me.

PILGRIM IN TRAINING

In the swimming pool,
I dodge toddler-clutching moms
floating toward me,
around the circular kiddie river.
They don't see—
as I water-walk against the current,
every sturdy press of knee and foot,
knee and foot, each push
against unseen waves—
this granny's climbing the Pyrenees.

In Sync

Hard to explain *churros'* quintessence,
not the fried dough at carnivals,
not greasy, not oversweet donuts.

A sure cure for jet lag,
cooked in virgin olive oil as you watch,
dipped in finest freshly-melted chocolate,

churros to roll in your mouth,
in the Churrería
near her brother's house in Madrid.

Tonguing visions of their crinkled crispiness,
lying in our bed,
I ponder aloud, trying to sound intelligent,

I wonder how chocolate originated,
did it enter Iberia with the Moors,
or later, from the New World?

When she exclaims,
I was just thinking of chocolate too,
we are so in sync!

I needn't say
what happens then—
her lips tasting even better

than *churros con chocolate,*
the kind we will have next week,
in her native Spain.

MADRE

As the train rumbles side to side,
as we leave the town of Clara's birth,
we move into the hot, dry plain,
green after recent, sweet spring rains—
remembering how we sat
in her mother's flat, abode of fifty years,

as thunder sang its omen tones,
as clouds—dark grey against still-blue sky—
let go their load on us, on the city,
on all of Spain, a heavy rain—
and how today the sky's all sun,
swept clean after last night's weeping.

This morning we crossed
the not-yet busy street, as her mother
leaned over the balcony,
her small frame bent with age,
her spine *un perro rabioso que muerde*—
a rabid dog she can't bite back—

we and she called and waved,
as we turned the sunny corner,
our backpacks the last she sees of us,
as she turns away,
closing the casement window,
to sit alone and think of us.

RINSE AND REPEAT

In the birthplace of a saint,
we rest on a bench, ponchos
protecting us from rain.
Another town
of narrow stone streets,
spilling red, pink, and white geraniums,
cats transacting
mysterious feline business.
We hobble to a restaurant,
remove shoes, rub our feet,
to ease twenty miles hiked.
Eat a pilgrim meal
inspired by peasants.
No need for much talk—
momentarily, we'll sleep,
to sounds of children
playing in the street.
Before dawn, we're ready
to do it all over again.

In Estella

The pain in my knee
begs me to stop for the day,
wants me to fly home in defeat.
I crumple into a bus stop seat,
bus once a day, but just then,
round the bend, it materializes,
driver asking me to pray for him
when I arrive in Santiago
de Compostela, consoling
this limping, weeping,
non-Spanish-speaking pilgrim,
taking his bus off its route,
straight to an *Albergue* heaven,
where I sleep for two days,
and the knee quiets, allows me to go
four hundred miles more,
to do as I promised
the angel from Estella.

BELL JOURNAL

A wedding at two walks through
rose petals strewn on cobblestones,
a funeral comes and goes,
solemn family in their finest,
festive crowds at night,
who dance and sing and drink,
as the church bell tolls
the quarter-hour, each half,
and each whole: time noted
temporally, and constantly,
as we, weary pilgrims,
windows open to the Plaza,
breathe in Santo Domingo's life,
all through the night.

BELIEF

Walking the endless *Meseta,* we turn to see
yellow broom flowers, orange poppies going by—
the only way to know these pilgrims' progress.

Each night, an ancient town new to us,
steps closer to our journey's end—
we feel no mystic pull toward Santiago,

but we believe in the awe of those who do,
as Gregorian chants pipe through a darkened church,
and a friend we meet weeps freely at a café table.

We leave Castrojeriz in the graying dark,
before dawn, before cafés open, our shoes
tapping a slow rhythm on quiet streets,

and though at this moment they're empty of all but us,
we know the road, the path we've chosen,
takes us somewhere many have gone before.

We feel them all in the hard-packed trail,
in our aching feet,
in our will to keep going, a mysticism we can believe.

WHAT WAS THE BEST CUP OF COFFEE?

At the top of the mesa, that early morning in the rain.

What is it, to walk every day through a foreign land, follow yellow arrows along an ancient path?

A time away from time, a slow movement of legs, a collection of folks you meet, fellow seekers, along the month-long way.

What about the coffee, why that one stop?
Because it was generous, unexpected, that man standing in the rain; because we were already weary, in spite of the day just beginning.

Did you think of yourself as a pilgrim?
It felt right to walk through stone towns, over rose petals strewn in front of relics, sit in dark churches. The locals liked us, even in the cities, even in our much-worn clothing, our backpacks, our obvious weariness. They dubbed us Pilgrims, and we accepted.

What about the problems?
Every moment felt right, even when the washing machines took our coins, the nights we couldn't find food, all part of the project of making our way like snails across the map of Spain.

What Did You Discover?
Every day, every step led to changes we could see. It would start to rain, then the rain would subside, a mountain would loom in front of us, then we were on the top, a knee would ache, then the pain would stop. By the end, how strong we came to feel; how quiet inside.

MUD

After the steep climb,
after the *Camino Angel* on top,
proffering coffee, hot milk, rolls,
after the long trudge across the high mesa,
in the cloudy, wet dawn,
we braved the steep descent,
the path slippery with stones,
left knee starting to ache, and just
when we thought it would be easy,
the path flattening to a road,
ribboning beyond sight—we found
not ease, but deep squelch,
boot-sucking and red, each step
into wet glue weighing us down,
as we simply carried on,
as it started, once again, to rain,
a deeper test that plumbed a well
of un-guessed rebelliousness.

THE ROSES OF LOGROÑO

Among the roses of Logroño,
aging, aching limbs, weariness,
sense of homelessness—
even news of a good friend's death,
fade into nothingness,
in the presence of climbing blossoms
brightened by the sun
brushing clouds away,
by floating in scent,
sweet on the tongue as honey,
amid church bells'
constant tolling,
beneath the fragrant roses
of Logroño.

Second Breakfast

Tortilla de patatas,
warm from the pan,
soft, but not runny,
local potatoes and eggs,
fresh bread on the side.
We hold a slice in one hand,
un café in the other,
leche divinely foamed—
so delicious each morning,
imbedded with gratitude,
after trudging six miles,
climbing steep mesas,
sliding down through the rain,
with no injury to claim.

OUR NAME

We were given the name,
as we sat defeated, weeping on a bus,
having given up for the day—
given in a café, faces bright
and eager before dawn,
backpacks slung by our sides,
collapsed, resting in shade,
given leaning over a bridge,
limping to vespers, to save aching knees,
given crossing a wet poppy field,
toward others of our tribe,
having lost the way,
getting sick, roadside,
given striding through small towns,
locals running out, saluting us, calling us
by our given name—*Pilgrim,*
requesting that we bless them,
as if persisting in the suffering we chose,
gave us a saintly aura.

IMAGINE

Today, someone rose
even earlier than we,
a woman in long skirts,
bending to collect juicy,
fat snails, apron full
of someone's lunch,
caracoles with garlic,
saffron, in steaming
broth, in *paella,* savory
tapa de caracoles,
feasts we'll imagine
hours later as we munch
granola bars like packed
sawdust, somewhere
further along our dusty path.

BACK TO SAND: AT THE MONASTERY OF SAN FÉLIX DE OCA

Swallows dart through open window holes,
in a hurry to make their summer nests.

Eager grass sprouts among broken rocks,
fallen bits of mortar turning slowly back to sand.

A tomb remains, a name inscribed in stone,
honoring love lost a thousand years ago.

We mouth the words, honor the couple with a kiss,
admire two tenacious snails clinging to wet grass spears—

just beginning to shake in rising wind,
black clouds mobbing to drench us yet again.

We pull our jackets close around our chests,
and journey on,

wondering who will mark our passing,
even ten years hence.

RABÉ DE LAS CALZADAS

The buildings are limestone,
rosy, ochre, ancient blocks,
the church is stone,
on top an iron cross.

In a rooftop nest
of wheat and twigs
she's gathered from the field,
a stork on skinny legs
stretches her wings
and feeds her young.

A church bell chimes the hour
and the quarter hour
and the half
as seeds float down from unseen trees—
linden, oak, acacia, birch.

A small black dog trots by,
at home in this ancient town,
as are the storks, the seeds,
the iron lamps,
the oval drinking trough,
the wind holes cut in stone.

In Léon, After Three Weeks of Rain

These clean children parading
cobbled streets to school,
these pigeons hoping for a crumb,
ready for the day as we.

These pilgrims passing on the trail
in slant morning light,
saluting us in fellowship.

These moments I would slow,
if I could, absorbing more deeply
the sun's healing.

In Herrerías

This late spring afternoon,
among the mountains of Léon,
I sit and watch the light
moving on a shadowed field,
like the finger of fate,
rounded bales of still-green hay,
poplar leaves shuddering
like penitents receiving grace,
in the breeze cooling my face,
the usual shadows
lengthening toward night—
but in the woods, unseen, a bird
I've never heard before—
a call arising from ancient tales,
a strangely plangent, medieval song,
but so clear, right here: *Cuckoo.*
I rub my ears, and hear again:
Cuckoo, cuckoo, cuckoo—
and then, *Sumer is icumen in*
rising through time-woods in my mind,
from elementary school, my singing
coo coo coo coo, loudly sing cuckoo,
in concord with these Spanish woods.

A TABLE ON THE GRASS, NÁJERA

Thanks be for this place of rest,
mid-way through our trek,
this table placed on grass,
café with river view, parade passing,
drums and lively song,
above the muddy, rain-fed waters.
Thanks be for a week of climbing Pyrenees,
striding safely through lightning storms
in open fields, surviving constant drenching,
bone weariness, a day of violent illness.
Thanks be for the will to shoulder
backpacks once again, to rejoin
the holy pilgrim stream.
May we follow to the end,
grateful to our bodies and minds,
for letting spirit through.

A Walking Mantra to be Sung Toward the End of Each Day

We are weary pilgrims
with every step we take
on and on to Santiago
we don't know why
please tell us why…

Over hills and mountains
across the high Meseta
on muddy roads and hot dry paths
we don't know why
please tell us why…

Through the rain and thunder
beneath electric wires
over fields of poppies
we don't know why
please tell us why…

To the great Cathedral
with every step we take
on and on to Santiago
we don't know why
please tell us why…

NOTES

The Camino has its origins in the 9th century. In 812 the purported relics of St. James, one of Jesus' disciples, were found in a remote part of Northwestern Spain. According to legend or religious tradition, he had visited the region to spread the Gospel and, upon his death in Jerusalem, his followers returned to bury his body in a field. News of the discovery extended quickly and, by the 12th century, Santiago was one of three fundamental pilgrimage sites of Christendom (the others being Rome and Jerusalem). The shrine, later Cathedral, promised forgiveness of all sins to those who arrived at its doors.

Acknowledgments

Grateful acknowledgment is made to the editors of the journals and anthologies who first published the following poems. The poems, sometimes in earlier versions, appeared as follows:

Live Encounters: "In Herrerías," "Oh When the Saints," "Rabé de las Calzadas"

Muddy River Poetry: "Belief," "The First Stage," "The Return"

One Art Poetry: "A Hot Day in Madrid"

Prime Number Magazine: "Madre"

The Other Journal: "Back to Sand"

About the Author

Laura Foley is the author of seven poetry collections. *Why I Never Finished My Dissertation* (Headmistress Press) received a starred Kirkus Review and an Eric Hoffer Award. Her collection *It's This* is forthcoming from Salmon Press. Her poems have won numerous awards, and national recognition—read frequently by Garrison Keillor on *The Writers Almanac;* appearing in Ted Kooser's *American Life in Poetry.* Her poems have appeared in *Alaska Quarterly Review, Valparaiso Poetry Review, Poetry Society London, Crannog Magazine* (Ireland), *DMQ Review, Atlanta Review, Mason Street, JAMA,* and many others. Her work has been included in many anthologies such as: *Poetry of Presence: An Anthology of Mindfulness Poems, Healing the Divide: Poems of Kindness and Connection,* and *How to Love the World: Poems of Gratitude and Hope.*

Laura lives with her wife, Clara Gimenez, among the hills of Vermont. www.laurafoley.net

HEADMISTRESS PRESS BOOKS

Everything We Need - Laura Foley

Tender, Tender - Jessica Jewell

A Trickle of Bloom Becomes You - Jen Rouse

Cyborg Sister - Jackie Craven

Demoted Planet - Katherine Fallon

Earlier Households - Bonnie J. Morris

The Things We Bring with Us: Travel Poems - S.G. Huerta

The Water Between Us - Gillian Ebersole

Discomfort - Sarah Caulfield

The History of a Voice - Jessica Jopp

I Wish My Father - Lesléa Newman

Tender Age - Luiza Flynn-Goodlett

Low-water's Edge - Jean A. Kingsley

Routine Bloodwork - Colleen McKee

Queer Hagiographies - Audra Puchalski

Why I Never Finished My Dissertation - Laura Foley

The Princess of Pain - Carolyn Gage & Sudie Rakusin

Seed - Janice Gould

Riding with Anne Sexton - Jen Rouse

Spoiled Meat - Nicole Santalucia

Cake - Jen Rouse

The Salt and the Song - Virginia Petrucci

mad girl's crush tweet - summer jade leavitt

Saturn coming out of its Retrograde - Briana Roldan

i am this girl - gina marie bernard

Week/End - Sarah Duncan

My Girl's Green Jacket - Mary Meriam

Nuts in Nutland - Mary Meriam & Hannah Barrett

Lovely - Lesléa Newman

Teeth & Teeth - Robin Reagler

How Distant the City - Freesia McKee

Shopgirls - Marissa Higgins

Riddle - Diane Fortney

When She Woke She Was an Open Field - Hilary Brown

A Crown of Violets - Renée Vivien tr. Samantha Pious

Fireworks in the Graveyard - Joy Ladin

Social Dance - Carolyn Boll

The Force of Gratitude - Janice Gould

Spine - Sarah Caulfield

I Wore the Only Garden I've Ever Grown - Kathryn Leland

Diatribe from the Library - Farrell Greenwald Brenner

Blind Girl Grunt - Constance Merritt

Acid and Tender - Jen Rouse

Beautiful Machinery - Wendy DeGroat

Odd Mercy - Gail Thomas

The Great Scissor Hunt - Jessica K. Hylton

A Bracelet of Honeybees - Lynn Strongin

Whirlwind @ Lesbos - Risa Denenberg

The Body's Alphabet - Ann Tweedy

First name Barbie last name Doll - Maureen Bocka

Heaven to Me - Abe Louise Young

Sticky - Carter Steinmann

Tiger Laughs When You Push - Ruth Lehrer

Night Ringing - Laura Foley

Paper Cranes - Dinah Dietrich

On Loving a Saudi Girl - Carina Yun

The Burn Poems - Lynn Strongin

I Carry My Mother - Lesléa Newman

Distant Music - Joan Annsfire

The Awful Suicidal Swans - Flower Conroy

Joy Street - Laura Foley

Chiaroscuro Kisses - G.L. Morrison

The Lillian Trilogy - Mary Meriam

Lady of the Moon - Amy Lowell, Lillian Faderman, Mary Meriam

Irresistible Sonnets - ed. Mary Meriam

Lavender Review - ed. Mary Meriam